Read[illegible]evise:

Over 170 Daily Revisi[illegible] Mini-Lessons

Connie Prevatte

Rigby Best Teachers Press

An imprint of Rigby

Dedication
To Sam . . . and other children beginning their journey into the world of writing.

For more information about other books from Rigby Best Teachers Press, please contact Rigby at 800-822-8661 or visit **www.rigby.com**

Editor: Julia Moses and Mary Susnis
Executive Editor: Georgine Cooper
Designer: Nancy Rudd
Design Project Manager: Tom Sjoerdsma
Cover Illustrator: Terry Sirrell

06 05 04
10 9 8 7 6 5 4 3 2

Printed in the United States of America.

ISBN 0-7578-2103-0
Ready, Set, Revise: Over 170 Daily Revision Mini-Lessons

Contents

Word Usage

Sentences

Transition

Contents

Setting

Character

Contents

Hooks

Closure

Point of View

Dialogue

Plot

Contents

Elaboration

Introduction

Writing, conferencing, and revising are all necessary components of the writing lesson; however, the time to complete these activities is limited. If the goal is writing success, then it is necessary to provide a writing environment that allows time for these components. This type of writing environment provides you with the opportunity to instruct students in the art of writing.

Creating successful writing experiences is the goal of writing instruction.

Success occurs when:

- **Students love writing and feel empowered as authors.**
- **Students' writing is interesting, informative, focused, imaginative, and vivid.**
- **Students score at proficiency or above proficiency as measured on state-mandated writing tests.**

Ready, Set, Revise is an instructional tool that contributes to effective writing instruction. It will help you to help your students sharpen their writing skills. You can foster the love of writing by sharing examples of excellent writing from children's literature. In some instances, popular children's literature has been used as a foundation for *Ready, Set, Revise.*

Writing Class Format

Students need writing instruction daily. The 40-45 minute writing class format consists of four distinct components:

Editing Mini-Lesson	**3 to 5 minutes**
Revision Mini-Lesson	**4 to 8 minutes**
Writing Process	**22 to 28 minutes**
Sharing	**Last 5 minutes**

Choose the mini-lesson based on the needs of your students. Select your daily lesson from the following categories:

 **Word Usage**

 **Sentences**

 **Transition**

 **Setting**

 **Character**

 **Hooks**

 **Closure**

 **Point of View**

 **Dialogue**

 **Plot**

 **Elaboration**

Procedure

The 4- to 8- Minute Mini-Lesson

Step 1: You teach.
Step 2: Students do (collaboratively).
Step 3: Students share (whole group).

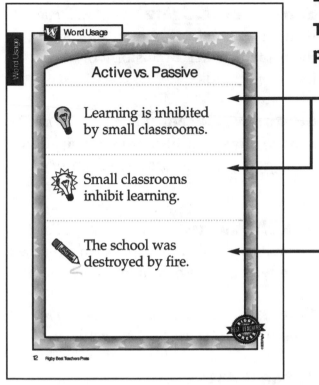

Word Usage

Active vs. Passive

Learning is inhibited by small classrooms.

Small classrooms inhibit learning.

The school was destroyed by fire.

12 Rigby Best Teachers Press

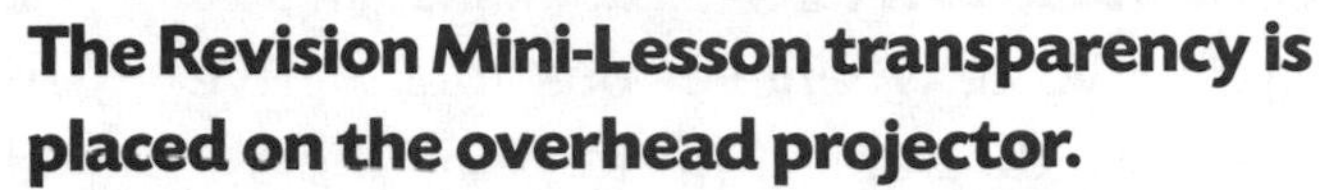

The Revision Mini-Lesson transparency is placed on the overhead projector.

Step 1—Briefly present the concept to the whole class. Discuss the quality of the first sentence and compare it to the second sentence or discuss the writing techniques used in the model. Stick to one or two main points that students can understand.

Step 2—Students work in collaborative groups, applying their knowledge to revise the Student Challenge.

Step 3—Each collaborative group shares their revision with the whole class to illustrate the range of possible revisions.

Mini-lessons are marked with the following icons to guide students' attention. Before using the transparencies, review each icon. You may want to make a copy of the information below for each student's writing folder or to post in your room.

Initial Sentence—This icon signals an initial sentence. This type of sentence may appear commonly in student writings. It is not necessarily wrong, but it is an example of a sentence that can be revised to be more effective.

Revised Sentence—This icon signals a revision of the initial sentence.

Model—This icon represents a sentence that provides an example of the skill to practice.

Student Challenge— This icon represents the type of sentence that may appear commonly in writing. It is not necessarily wrong, but it is an example of a sentence that can be revised to be more effective.

Word Usage Teaching Points

Use active voice whenever possible. Active voice shows the subject performing the action, rather than the action happening to the subject.

Enhancing the image requires a writer to visualize more graphically.

"Get" and "got" are overused. Brainstorm other more descriptive verbs to replace them.

The word "thing" leaves a lot to the imagination. Encourage students to name and describe "things."

Replace weak verbs with more interesting action words.

Replace common nouns with proper nouns to give writing more clarity.

Description evokes sensory experiences.

Describe textures, temperatures, and other tactile impressions so the reader feels the same sensations.

Non-judgmental description allows the reader to infer. Brainstorm other judgment words.

Readers draw conclusions based on strong descriptions. Brainstorm other sensory words.

Consult a thesaurus to replace an overused word with a more entertaining one.

Similes use "like" or "as" to compare.

"You should know" and "you should understand" are common phrases that keep writers from getting to the point. Take out unnecessary phrases.

Use direct and explicit adjectives whenever possible. Avoid using the negatives, "no" and "not."

Metaphors help the writer create imagery. Metaphors compare things using the words, "is," "was," "are," or "were."

Personification gives human characteristics to non-human things.

Active vs. Passive

Learning is inhibited by small classrooms.

Small classrooms inhibit learning.

The school was destroyed by fire.

Enhance the Image

The rain came down on us.

The rain, pouring down in sheets, drenched us from head to toe.

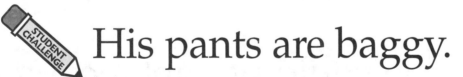

His pants are baggy.

To Get

earn   acquire   obtain   procure

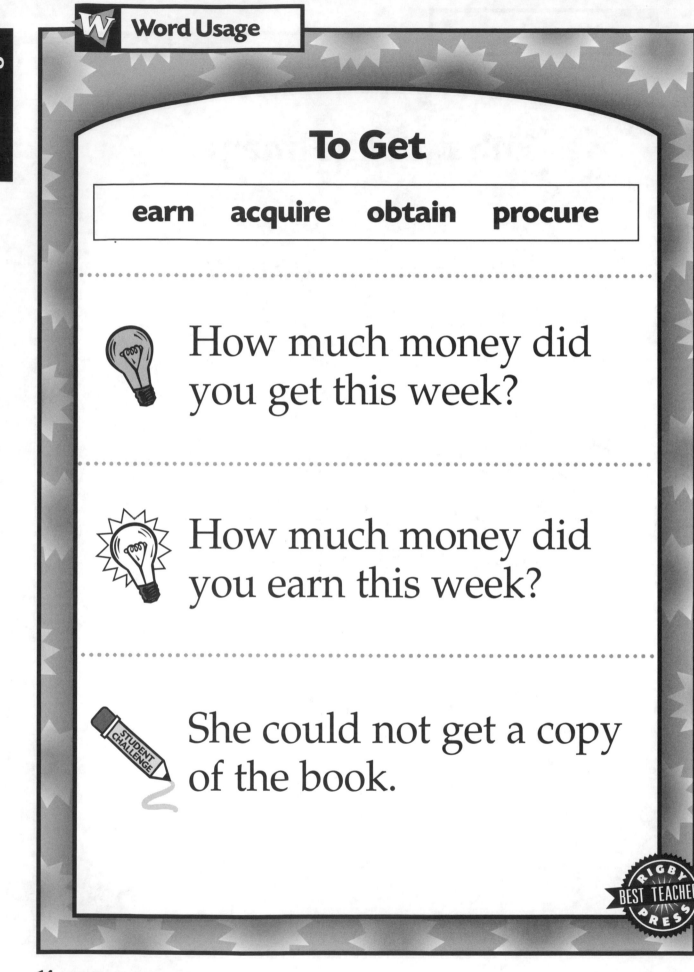

How much money did you get this week?

How much money did you earn this week?

She could not get a copy of the book.

The Thing

The thing was in her hair.

The yellow bow was in her hair.

Mary lost the thing in her coat pocket.

W Word Usage

Interesting Verbs

She walked slowly and aimlessly toward the door.

She wandered toward the door.

Tom spoke softly to his brother.

Proper Nouns

Steven vacationed in the mountains.

Steven vacationed in Denali National Park in Alaska.

Jane loves to go to the beach.

Word Usage

Sensory Words: Smell

The pillows smelled bad.

The odor of the pillows, musty with age, invaded my nostrils.

The school cafeteria smells weird.

Word Usage

Sensory Words: Touch

My feet were wet.

My toes curled as the spilled fruit juice seeped into the worn corners of my shoes.

The beach was sandy.

W Word Usage

Sensing vs. Judging

Judgmental Words:
awful, silly, attractive, ugly, lovely, kind, tremendous, wonderful, good

Sensory Words:
warm, chalky, soft, squirming, loud, sharp

Sam is a silly little boy.

Sam, a squirming little boy, climbed over the table.

It was a very good lunch.

Sensing vs. Judging 2

Judgmental Words:
terrible, foolish, beautiful, homely, pretty, pleasant, amazing, marvelous

Sensory Words:
white, milky, rough, bright, wiggling, pointy

Mrs. Fine is a nice teacher.

Mrs. Fine's bright smile quickened as she glided down the hallway, winking at former students.

The car was big.

The Thesaurus

Large: enormous, huge, tall, giant

She lives in a big house.

She lives in an enormous house.

Tom is a small boy.

Similes

Meagan is pretty.

Meagan is as pretty as a dewdrop on a rose petal.

Kyle is tired.

W Word Usage

To the Point

You should understand that eating right and exercising is good for your health.

Eating right and exercising are healthy.

You should know that you cannot get good grades without working hard.

RIGBY BEST TEACHERS PRESS

Avoid the Negative

Her face was not clean.

Her face was smudged with dirt.

The lunch was not good.

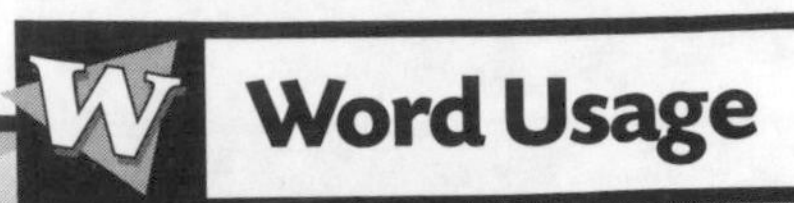

Metaphors

Grandmother's smile is kind.

Grandmother's smile is the sunshine that warms my day.

The tornado was destructive.

Personification

The stars are shining.

The stars wink mischievously at me.

The wind makes noise.

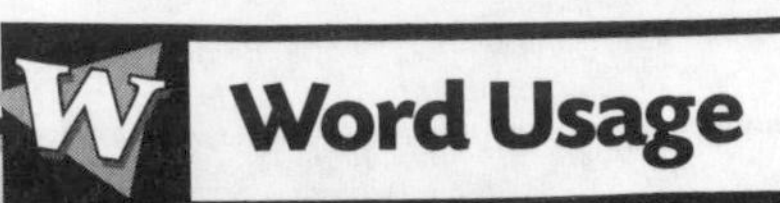

Avoid Clichés

It rained cats and dogs.

The rain fell in relentless torrents.

He is as light as a feather.

Fact vs. Opinion: Shades of Meaning

Fact: He is tall.

Positive Opinion:
He is graceful.

Negative Opinion:
He is gawky.

Fact: Sean is young.

Positive Opinion:

Negative Opinion:

Product Names

Alliteration: Tons of Toys

Pun: A Cut Above (beauty salon)

Rhyme: Deals on Wheels (bike store)

Invent product names for: bubble gum, a bookstore, marbles, kite shop, an umbrella, or popcorn.

Alliteration:

Pun:

Rhyme:

Titles Matter

Emotional Words:
Tears on the Land

The One-Word Title: *Redwall*

Characters: *Maniac Magee*

Setting: *Where the Wild Things Are*

Problem: *There's a Boy in the Girls' Bathroom*

Object: *Charlotte's Web*

Create a title in each category for a story about a boy and girl lost in the woods.

Emotional Words	Setting
The One-Word Title	Problem
Characters	Object

RIGBY BEST TEACHERS PRESS

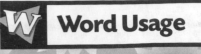

W Word Usage

Specific Language

Her pretty hair glistened in the sun.

Her thick, chestnut hair glistened in the sun.

The fancy car drove past our house.

Sentences Teaching Points

Sentences

Sentences

Making Connections

Maggie is a quiet student. She has green eyes. Her blond hair is long. Freckles cover her face.

Maggie is a quiet student with lovely green eyes. Her long blond hair frames her freckled face.

Juan is a great athlete. He likes to play football. He also likes running track.

RIGBY BEST TEACHERS PRESS

Sentence Expanding

The jet flies.

The supersonic jet flies above the city toward the clouds.

The painting is beautiful.

Sentence Expanding 2

The dog chased me.

My hair stood on end as the snarling dog chased me down the alley.

His sweater was torn.

Sentence Expanding 3

The book is old.

The corners of the book were frayed with age.

The room was messy.

Using Staccato Sentences To Create Tension

The blue box was sitting on the teacher's desk and began to move. I wondered what was inside.

The blue box was sitting on the teacher's desk. It moved. Then it moved again. My heart thumped. What was inside?

I picked up the bottle that was covered with sand. I looked inside and heard a small voice.

Parallelism

The party will begin if the class is quiet and the aisles are clean, and work must be completed.

The party will begin when the class is quiet, the aisles are clean, and the work is completed.

She ran into the house, went up the stairs, and is jogging down the hall.

RIGBY BEST TEACHERS PRESS

Sentences

There Is, There Are

There are many students who will benefit from the new gym.

Many students will benefit from the new gym.

There is a lot of pressure placed on students to make good grades.

RIGBY BEST TEACHERS PRESS

Combine Sentences to Link Ideas

The thunderstorm downed trees and left the city without electricity. The restoration may take several days.

Restoring electricity may take several days the after thunderstorms knocked down trees and left the city without power.

The entire sixth-grade class is looking forward to summer vacation. They will be going to the beach.

Combine Sentences to Link Ideas 2

Students need recess. It provides an opportunity to talk with friends. Recess provides an opportunity to improve athletic ability.

Recess not only provides students an opportunity to talk with friends, it provides an opportunity to improve athletic ability.

Apples are good for you. They have vitamins your body needs. Apples are a good source of fiber.

Participles

Matt turned in his homework and felt his spirits soar.

Turning in his homework, Matt felt his spirits soar.

Jordan scored his third goal and won the game for his team.

RIGBY BEST TEACHERS PRESS

Sentences

Appositives

The band played songs that everyone enjoyed.

The band, an upbeat group of teens, played songs that everyone enjoyed.

The skateboard raced down the hill and barely hung on to the pavement.

Absolutes

Wrinkled and gray-haired, she was obviously an elderly woman.

The peach was hard and sour. It was definitely not ripe.

Absolutes 2

Tail wagging, ears flapping, Sparky ran out to greet his best friend.

When the symphony ended, everyone leaped to their feet.

Begin with an Adverb

She entered the classroom quietly and found a seat in front.

Quietly she entered the classroom and found a seat in front.

David walked briskly through the hallway and ran into Mrs. Jersey.

Begin with a Prepositional Phrase

I could see the students working as I looked through the open window.

Through the open window, I could see the students working.

Mr. Smith ate lunch during the game.

Transition Teaching Points

Note: Posters of transition words may be helpful for use as classroom visuals.

Sequence Transitions

meanwhile	before	finally
soon	when	after awhile

First, the class read a story. Second, the class went to lunch. Third, the class took a test.

Before lunch the class read a story. When lunch was over, they took a test.

First, Mary got dressed for school. Second, she ate breakfast. Third, Mary boarded the bus.

RIGBY BEST TEACHERS PRESS

The Building Block Approach

Answer these questions:

Who?	**How?**	**Why?**
What?	**Where?**	**Results?**

At her teacher's insistence, Molly entered the Greenville Science Contest at her middle school. Her hard work paid off when she won first prize and was asked to represent her school at the state finals.

Create a paragraph using the building block approach.

Movement Transitions

below	above	just beyond
nearby	to the left	away from

Allison lived *near* Charlotte. Her house was in a small quiet neighborhood just *beyond* the city limits. She could play ball in *front* of her house.

Create a paragraph using movement.

Movement Transitions 2

under	**near**	**to the right**
opposite	**across**	**in the background**
adjacent to	**beyond**	**further**

The rabbit ran *under* the bush to hide. He could hear leaves fluttering *across* the field.

Use transitional words to connect two objects.

Transition

Time Transitions

after	**now**	**subsequently**
afterward	**until**	**meanwhile**
as soon	**not long after**	**soon**
finally	**when**	**yesterday**
later	**while**	**tomorrow**

Dad took a nap. Sally wrapped the gift.

After dinner, Dad took a nap. *In the meantime,* Sally wrapped the gift.

Sam played ball. Ashley cooked dinner.

Time Transitions 2

now	**when**
before	**until**
immediately	**once**
in the meantime	**at**
at the same time	**as**

I played in the school band.
Then I played basketball.

Before I played basketball,
I played in the school band.

Write a sentence that tells when you played hockey and when you were on the golf team.

RIGBY BEST TEACHERS PRESS

Transition

Expository Transitions

furthermore	in fact	consequently
moreover	to illustrate	accordingly
also	in conclusion	for this reason
besides	in summary	to begin with
similarly	in other words	however
for example	therefore	although
equally important	finally	
for instance	as a result	

Eating balanced, nutritious meals is important for good health. *Equally important*, are proper rest and exercise.

Use a transition to link two facts.

Transitions That Add Information

and	**moreover**	**second**
also	**again**	**along with**
in addition	**further**	**besides**
finally	**furthermore**	

Rebecca led a campaign to bring recycling to our community. Marcus helped her.

Rebecca, with Marcus's help, led a campaign to bring recycling to our community.

I do well on most spelling tests. I like to read.

RIGBY BEST TEACHERS PRESS

Transitions That Show Contrast

although	**on the other hand**
still	**but**
nevertheless	**however**
after all	**whereas**

The seventh grade students set a school-wide example for citizenship this year. They are not a popular group.

Although the seventh grade students set a school-wide example for citizenship this year, they are not a popular group.

Jennifer skates very well. Donna doesn't.

Transitions That Emphasize

indeed	**again**	**so**
certainly	**in any event**	**truly**
in fact	**surely**	**for this reason**

I have been saving all my money from my summer job. *In fact,* I have enough to buy a new big screen TV.

Martin usually stays up late. He is often late for school.

Transitions That Give Examples

for instance	**as an illustration**
for example	**thus**
specifically	

Diane is one of our best players. *For instance,* she scored more points in our last two games than all other players combined .

Lucy is a good friend. She helps people even when it is not convenient for her.

Place Transitions

there	**beyond**	**above**
near	**here**	**below**
adjacent to	**opposite**	

My school's basketball team practices in the field *adjacent to* the band room.

Use a transition to show the location of the school and the park.

Conclusion Transitions

because	**as a result**	**naturally**
therefore	**it follows that**	**thus**
accordingly	**consequently**	

My class won the reading contest. *As a result*, we all received a homework pass.

Alex broke his arm. His handwriting is messy.

Comparison Transitions

likewise	**unlike**
relative to	**on the other hand**
in common with	**conversely**
similarly	**as opposed to**
just as	

Apes are very protective of their offspring. *Similarly,* alligator mothers ferociously defend their eggs.

Compare two things, people, actions, or places.

Transition

Teaching Points

Tone

Humor:

Awaiting my first lesson,
I looked at the swimming pool.
Do kids really swim without flippers?

Optimism:

Awaiting my first lesson,
I looked at the swimming pool.
I could hardly wait to begin.

Finish this paragraph.

Fear:

Awaiting my first lesson,
I looked at the swimming pool.

RIGBY BEST TEACHERS PRESS

Description of Time: Historical Period

Consider the following when writing about a historical period.

clothing	**technology**
transportation	**appliances**

Margo smoothed her bell-bottoms and stroked the peace symbol on her necklace.

Brainstorm what you know about the 1800s in the American West. Write a setting sentence using your ideas.

Description of Season Through Clothing

Jason's shorts and T-shirt clung to his back as he stepped outside onto the blistering pavement.

Describe a season with clothing.

Description of Season

Matthew tucked the gift securely under his arm and made his way up the icy sidewalk. He didn't notice the carolers or even the man in the Santa suit ringing the Salvation Army bell.

Describe a season.

Description of Weather

Consider the following when describing weather.

snow	**temperature**	**wind**
rain	**fog**	**cloud cover**

Thunder boomed and lightning forked across the sky. We had no idea how much further we had to go.

Describe the weather.

Time of Day

Consider the following when describing the time of day.

sunrise/sunset
late afternoon
"inky dark"
noon
twilight
eating breakfast
eating lunch

Jerry gobbled the last bit of burnt toast laden with strawberry jam.

Describe a time of day.

Atmosphere

Laura's fingers brushed the cobwebbed corners, and she felt a sudden chill in the air.

Create an atmosphere of excitement, happiness, or fear.

Words for Familiar Settings

Bedroom:

crib, bed, window, comforter, television, dresser, alarm clock, night stand

Brainstorm words for these settings:

kitchen
living room
bathroom
classroom

Words for Unfamiliar Settings

Closet:

hangers, belts, clothes, shoe boxes

Brainstorm words for these settings:

refrigerator
toy box
parked car

Setting

Words for Fantasy Settings

Castle:
turret, moat, throne, stone walls, goblets, torches

Brainstorm words for these settings:

dungeon
spacecraft
ant hill
ship

Change the Setting

Consider the following setting changes for these popular stories.

Cinderella	**Your town**
Jack and the Beanstalk	**Old West**
Hansel & Gretel	**The beach**
Sleeping Beauty	**Hollywood**

Cinderella was startled by the school bell ringing to signal the stroke of midnight. Once more she glanced at Coach Charming and then ran from the gymnasium. In her rush, Cinderella left a size 8 sneaker sitting on the stairs of Princeville High.

Write a scene from one of the stories above. Change the setting.

Setting

Ambience

Consider such qualities as the following when creating ambience.

Sound: volume, sharpness
Smell: sweetness, intensity
Touch: texture, temperature
Sight: color, brightness, size, shape

Aunt Stacey's cottage on Jewel Lake reminds me of an oil painting I saw once. Everything is toned down, softened by time. Even the sunlight filtering through the trees seems different from the light that shines on the city. The afternoon's warm golden glow makes you want to take a long nap on one of her old puffy sofas.

Create the ambience of a setting.

Character Teaching Points

Character Description Through Setting

For fifteen years, Duncan had lived inside Starling Castle. That was his whole life. Knowing he would probably never live anywhere else made Duncan long for a life far away—a life where he was not King.

Create a setting to illustrate a lonely character.

Character Description Through Word Pictures

Susanna is a little girl.
She turned cartwheels.

Susanna, a perky, frivolous little girl, turned cartwheels on her shoestring legs.

John is a quiet boy.
He is also very short.

Character Description Through Facial Expressions

Julie was sad.

Julie's eyes filled with tears, and her lips trembled.

Derek was happy.

Character Description Through Gestures

Kristen was upset.

Flailing her arms, Kristen ranted about the new coach.

Tom was scared.

Character Description Through Unconscious Movements

John was bored.

John's drummed his fingers against the desktop as he eyed the clock.

Patti was worried.

Character Description Through Reactions to Stress

Paul is irritated.

Paul tripped over the chair. He muttered under his breath and threw down his books. How could he have failed that test?

Sarah is shy.

Character Description Through Character Traits

Consider the following traits when describing characters.

cold	**friendly**
unselfish	**greedy**
calculating	**suspicious**

David is an unfriendly person.

David ignored Claire and marched past her, even though she smiled at him.

Sarah is a selfish person.

Character

Character Description Through Speech

Polite:

"Spaghetti and milk, please. I'd appreciate it if you would hurry. I'm late for class."

Rude:

"Give me spaghetti and milk. Hurry up—I'm late for class."

Write dialogue to portray a shy character in the situation as above.

Character Description Through Clothing

He was a fussy little boy.

He didn't like to get his clothes messy, and whenever his shirt was wrinkled, he would cry.

She is a tomboy.

Nobody's Pefect

Steven is an A student and an all-star quarterback. He welcomed the new student and introduced him around.

Steven is an A student and an all-star quarterback. He welcomed the new student and introduced him around. Then he began to worry. The new student was too smart, maybe smarter than Steven.

Create a character who is good, but experiences internal conflict.

RIGBY BEST TEACHERS PRESS

Character Description Through Conflict

Jane is lazy. Maria is ambitious.

Conflict: Maria wants her class to win the spelling competition. Jane refuses to study.

Sam is not athletic. Greg is the star of the soccer team.

Write a conflict that shows the traits of these characters.

Character Description Through Transformation

Mark always follows the rules. Greg spends most of his time in the principal's office.

The transformation:
Mark realizes Greg gets into trouble to avoid reading. He teaches Greg to read, and Greg becomes a model student.

Don is the most popular boy in class. Janet is the class wallflower.

Create the transformation that shows the traits of these characters.

Intrinsic Qualities: Emotional

Consider the following when describing characters.

dramatic
sad
insecure
shy
optimistic
pessimistic
quarrelsome
cautious

Happy:
smiling face, springy walk, sparkling eyes, vivacious voice

Select an emotional intrinsic quality and write descriptors.

Character

Intrinsic Qualities: Intellectual

Consider the following when describing characters.

curious
smart
imaginative
inventive
creative
resourceful

Smart:
hand always raised,
nose in a book,
extensive vocabulary

Select an intellectual intrinsic quality and write descriptors.

Intrinsic Qualities: Social

Consider the following when describing characters.

bossy	**leader**
reserved	**follower**
overbearing	**cooperative**

Bossy:
hands on hips, wagging finger, always something to say

Select a social intrinsic quality and write descriptors.

Character

Extrinsic Qualities: Physical Appearance

Consider the following when describing characters.

height	**freckles**
weight	**scars**
hair color and style	**glasses**
eye color	**teeth**
brows	**hands**

Frazzled gray hair frames Mrs. Jones' heavily lined face.

Describe the looks of a five-month-old baby.

Extrinsic Qualities: Clothing

Consider the following clothing options when describing characters.

job related	**new**
casual	**old**
formal	**stylish**

Mr. Smith's polyester plaid pants clashed with his red striped shirt. The white wing tip shoes did not improve his overall look.

Use clothing to describe extrinsic qualities of a rock star or other type of musician.

Extrinsic Qualities: Habits

Consider habits like the following when describing characters.

squint	**chew on hair**
twitch	**push glasses up on nose**
bite lip	**hum**
crack knuckles	**shrug**

While Maggie glared at him, Jason bit his lip and looked around nervously.

Write a sentence using a character habit.

Extrinsic Qualities: Speech

Consider the following aspects of speech when describing characters.

speed
phrase usage
pitch
accent
dialect
volume

"That'll be quite enough out of you," Mary Margaret declared.

Write a descriptor using an aspect of a character's speech.

Non-Human Character Description

Tail wagging, tongue drooling, Boomer put his paw on my knee. "You're a good friend, Boomer," I said.

Describe a non-human character.

Hooks Teaching Points

Question Hooks

If people can act like animals, can animals act like people?

or

What could have happened to Josh?

Write a question hook.

Dialogue Hooks

"We are about to embark on a journey, gentleman, that may change the course of history," Captain Haywood announced.

or

"I know it was here this morning," Lorna whispered.

Write a hook using dialogue.

Fact Hooks

There are more than 3,000 species of frogs.

or

The United States grew quickly in the 1800s.

Write a fact hook.

Setting Hooks

They say Paula Payton lives under the bridge.

or

Jesse lay on the bank remembering too late not to get grass stains on his shirt.

Write a hook using setting.

Action Hooks: The Arrival

A few minutes after eleven, Amelia emerged from Principal Tyrone's office looking slightly bewildered.

or

The mailcarrier delivered a letter and an oversized, brown paper package to the last house on Elm Street.

Write a hook using the action of an arrival.

Action Hooks: The Departure

Without a penny in his pocket, Stryker left the tiny village of Chocowinity.

or

I stood staring at the rope swing as my dad backed out of the driveway and out of my life.

Write a hook using the action of a departure.

Action Hooks: Events in Progress

Tamok sprinted across the field and rolled down the embankment. "Hurry up! They're starting without us." he shouted.

or

The ball soared through the air awaiting the crack of the bat.

Write a hook using the action of an event in progress.

RIGBY BEST TEACHERS PRESS

Hyperbole Hooks

Charlie awoke with a pain like an elephant sitting on his chest.

or

My mom says I've made Mount Everest out of a molehill.

Write a hook using hyperbole.

Onomatopoeia Hooks

Thwack! Before I knew what had hit me, I was lying flat on my back.

or

Clang, clang, clang. The ship bell signaled our arrival in America.

Write a hook using onomatopoeia.

Sentence Fragment Hooks

"Where is the—?" Bailey knew in her heart that she was too late.

or

"I can't wait to try out my new—hey, it's missing a wheel!" Ryan whined.

Create a hook using a sentence fragment.

Character Hooks

James Henry is no ordinary boy, and his is no ordinary story.

or

I don't know why, but the first thing people say when they meet me is, "What's with your hair?"

Create a character hook.

Assorted Hooks

Question	**Onomatopoeia**
Dialogue	**Action**
Fact	**Character**
Setting	**Sentence fragment**
Hyperbole	

Look in other text for examples of hooks. What kinds did you find?

Closure Teaching Points

Climactic Ending

As they reached the top of the dune, Gillian and Robert beheld the limitless desert in front of them. "Come on," said Robert, "we've still got a long way to go."

Create a climactic ending.

Climactic Ending 2

The car picked up speed and plunged over the cliff toward the jagged rocks and sea below. Beth gasped, "They'll never survive that drop."

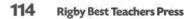

Create a climactic ending.

Cliffhanger Ending

"I didn't know he could climb the fence, Marty, honest. I'm sorry," Lee cried.

"It's okay, Lee. I'm sure he will be all right."

Create a cliffhanger ending.

Cliffhanger Ending 2

Next year the blue whales will have to move to an ocean that man hasn't polluted and that can sustain them—if one can be found.

Create a cliffhanger ending.

Future Action Ending

"A boa constrictor can be an excellent pet, Mom," she pleaded. "I swear I will take care of it. You won't even know it's here."

Create a future action ending.

Future Action Ending 2

If we don't concern ourselves with this, who will? I mean, it isn't every day someone tells you that you have the power to stop global warming. If we work together, I know we can make a difference.

Create a future action ending.

Ending with a Quotation

Aristotle best described debate when he said, "The fool persuades me with his reasons; the wise man persuades me with my own."

Create a quote closure.

Full-Circle Ending

Annie's eyes were riveted on the spot where she had to land precisely. "I can't do it," she thought...

Hitting her mark with precision, Annie heard the thunderous applause.

Create a full-circle ending.

Factual Ending

Recycling will make our valuable natural resources last longer.

or

Just because we can't see them, doesn't mean we aren't exposed to bacteria twenty-four hours a day.

Create a factual ending.

RIGBY BEST TEACHERS PRESS

All Kinds of Closure

Climactic Ending
Cliffhanger Ending
Future Action Ending
Ending with a Quotation
Full-Circle Ending
Factual Ending

Look for closures in various texts. What kinds did you find?

Point of View Teaching Points

First Person Narrative

My grandfather placed a stool next to his rocking chair, and I sat down on it beside him. I knew he had something important to tell me.

Create a scene. Use first person narrative.

Multiple Points of View

My sister Karen and I never do anything together anymore. It's not that we don't get along; it's just that she is too busy or has more important things to do.

I love my little sister Connie but she's only nine years old, and she doesn't have any idea what it's like to be in junior high.

Create a scene with multiple points of view.

Third Person Narrative

Malcolm still limped because of a childhood injury. As he walked into the class late again, Tonya worried. Now everyone would see his ungraceful entrance, and later they would tease him.

Create a narrative in third person.

Third Person Omniscient Subjective

Diane wondered if she was doing the right thing.

Create a sentence in third person omniscient subjective.

Point of View

Third Person Omniscient Objective

He grabbed the dirty rag and wiped his sweaty face.

Create a sentence in third person omniscient objective.

Who's Speaking?

First person:
I walked down the street.

Second person:
You walked down the street.

Third person:
He walked down the street.

Find a first, second, or third person point of view in text. Change it to another point of view.

Teaching Points

Instead of Said

exclaimed	**yelled**	**argued**
sighed	**whispered**	**wept**
moaned	**murmured**	**smirked**
screamed	**breathed**	**mumbled**

Look for other more descriptive verbs to replace "said." Write a dialogue sentence using a verb you found.

Instead of Shouted

argued	**snapped**
admonished	**ranted**
exclaimed	**wailed**
shrieked	**commanded**

Write a dialogue sentence using an alternative verb for shouted.

Speaking With Difficulty

sputtered	**choked**
stammered	**croaked**
gasped	**panted**

Write a dialogue using one of the words above to indicate that a person is having difficulty speaking.

Instead of Thought

wondered	**reflected**
considered	**pondered**
meditated	**contemplated**
reasoned	**reflected**

Write a dialogue sentence using an alternative verb for thought.

Who Is Talking?

Name: "No," said Maria.

Pronoun: "No," she said.

Describe: "No," the young student replied.

Looks: "No," the small, dark-haired girl replied.

Name: "Yes," said Mrs. Smith.

Pronoun:

Describe:

Looks:

Adding Dialogue

We marched around Aunt Martha's house.

"March with us, Aunt Martha!" I called, but she was closing her eyes and was remembering long ago.

Nicole and Joe sat in the cockpit of the small plane looking out across the sky.

Dialogue Enhances Action

He walked to the door and turned, "I will miss you, Sara."

or

Charles ran toward them crying, "Run for your lives!"

Write a dialogue action sentence.

Dialogue Enhances Action 2

The bear, ravenous and savage, burst through the tent. Ned stood transfixed. "It's going to get us, Dad," he wailed.

"Ned, get moving. Now!" Dad commanded.

Write dialogue to build action.

Dialogue

Enhance with Adverbs

"I finally made it to the Major League," Dan announced.

"I finally made it to the Major League," Dan announced proudly.

Marked murmured, "I don't know if I can make it over that bridge."

Dialogue

Dialogue To Develop Character

honest	**brave**
cowardly	**kind**
spoiled	**arrogant**

"You said I wouldn't have to stay here much longer," Jenny complained. "I'll never believe anything you say again!"

Pick one of the character traits above and write a dialogue sentence that shows how a character is feeling.

RIGBY BEST TEACHERS PRESS

With or Without Tension

Without Tension:

"Why are you late?" asked Greg.

"The traffic was heavy," replied Ashley.

With Tension:

"Why are you late?" quizzed Greg.

"I'm not late. You don't have to watch the clock. I can take care of myself," snapped Ashley.

Write dialogue with and without tension.

Teaching Points

The Plotting Game

The Protagonist:	Mrs. Graham
The Antagonist:	Cory, the mouse
The Setting:	School cafeteria
The Problem:	Cory terrifies students.
The Obstacles:	• Cory hides in a lunch box. • He gets stuck in a dishwasher. • He hides in Mrs. Graham's purse.
Foreshadow:	Mrs. Graham is lonely.
The Climax:	She finds Corey and realizes he is sweet and also lonely.

Play the plotting game.

Show Instead of Tell

Lola was happy when she got her bird as a present.

When Lola saw the bird's bright green feathers and beautifully colored tail, she shouted, "He's the most wonderful present ever!"

Juan was so eager to tell his mom all about the first day of school.

What's the Motivation?

jealousy	**anger**
fear	**grief**

Hannah doesn't want Dad to be friends with Joan, but I do. I like her, and she makes Dad happy. Hannah says she doesn't need a new mother, and she likes it when it's just the three of us without Joan.

Select a motivation and write a scene.

Plunge Right In

My alarm clock, boisterous and shrill, woke me with a start on that cool October morning.

or

Melanie's bike teetered on the edge of the massive hole.

Create a sentence that plunges right into the action of the story.

Plot

Description Adds Flair

Bailey noticed the cut on her arm as she lay in the grass. The wreck left her confused.

Bailey sat up, "Oh, my arm! It hurts so badly. I can't move it! How can I stop the bleeding?" she thought. "What happened to me? Why am I lying in the grass? Where's Jake? What happened to him?"

Bailey started to panic as she remembered the car turning over and over.

Write a scene with descriptive detail.

Event Pairing

Character:

Stranger leaning against the door

Captain Jared with hat pulled over ears

A small girl with pigtails carrying a backpack

Setting:

School bus

Sporting goods store

Sinking boat on a lake

Pair a character with a setting and write an event.

Decide the Plot

Conflict or Problem:
The box on the teacher's desk is moving.

Possible Plots:

- A puppy is hidden inside.
- A tiny talking mouse has sneaked into school.

Conflict or Problem:
The teacher's chair is missing.

Possible Plots:

Character Saves the Day

Aliens have invaded Earth and brought with them a virus that has no cure.

Samantha discovers an antidote and transports survivors to another world.

An earthquake will destroy the island where your character lives.

What does the character do?

Plot

Jeopardy

Main Conflict:
The character is lost in the desert.

Possible Ways Out:
- Find a compass.
- Discover a map.
- Be rescued by a Bedouin.

Create a plot based on this main conflict:
The character is trapped in a cave.

Possible Ways Out:

Plant the Seeds: Foreshadowing

Kyle walked through the unlocked door and sat down. He was unexpectedly nervous about something he couldn't quite express.

or

I never expect anyone to make a big fuss over my birthday. When you come from a large family like I do, you just get used to your birthday being like any other day.

Write a sentence that includes foreshadowing.

The Main Character Reacts

Boomer slipped beneath the ice. Sam saw his dog desperately trying to stay afloat.

Boomer slipped beneath the ice. Sam's heart beat wildly as he flung off his heavy down jacket and plunged into the river after his dog.

George watched as his best friend Joe was hit in the chest by a baseball.

RIGBY BEST TEACHERS PRESS

Evil Fails

Anna, a bully, teases other students and takes their belongings. She never seems to care what people think of her because she's so busy putting them down or getting them back. Anna ruined Tre's math book one day, and the teacher sent a note home. The next day Anna accused Tre of setting off the fire alarm, but witnesses came forward, and Anna was suspended from school.

Create a story about the failure of a character who does something wrong.

RIGBY BEST TEACHERS PRESS

Plot

Goodness Triumphs

Elaine was a little disappointed about not making the basketball team. "There were other girls who were better," she decided. When she saw Coach Marker coming down the hall toward her, her first instinct was to look the other way and ignore him. Instead, she forced herself to smile at him and in a cheerful voice said, "Hello, Coach Marker."

Surprisingly, he smiled back and replied, "Hi, Elaine. I was just looking for you. Another spot just opened up on the basketball team. I think you have great athletic ability, and you showed excellent sportsmanship. Are you still interested in playing?"

Create a story about a character who triumphs after doing something good.

Break the Stereotype

Conflict:
A football has just broken Mr. Smith's front window.

Who Did It?

angry principal	thug
trouble-maker	school cheerleader
shy student	class president

He ran to the window just in time to see Susan, the captain of the cheerleading squad, running away.

The essay was the finest Mrs. Potter had ever seen in the history of the essay contest.

Who Did It?

the class clown	an athlete
a trouble maker	a teacher

Flashback: Remembering

Flashbacks can be inner thoughts that focus on memories.

Eric rubbed his hands together and continued waiting for the bus. He thought about how warm the cozy diner had been.

or

Olivia sat on the porch swing. She smiled to herself thinking about her wedding. What a beautiful fall day it had been.

Create a flashback in which a character remembers a past event.

Flashback: The Actual Experience

Flashbacks can be an actual scene from the past.

He remembered how John had played the drums incredibly, his hands moving quickly and strongly. "You're amazing!" was all he had said.

Create a flashback recreating an actual scene.

Flashback Technique: Hinge Statements

The Initial Hinge:

She thought back. "I was so sick. My body felt limp and my temperature was high."

The Hinge Swing:

Now, a week later, she was feeling better than ever.

Create an initial hinge and the hinge swing.

Plot Development: Conflict in the Narrative

1	2	3	4
Minor Conflict	**Unhappy Resolution**	**Major Conflict**	**Happy Resolution**

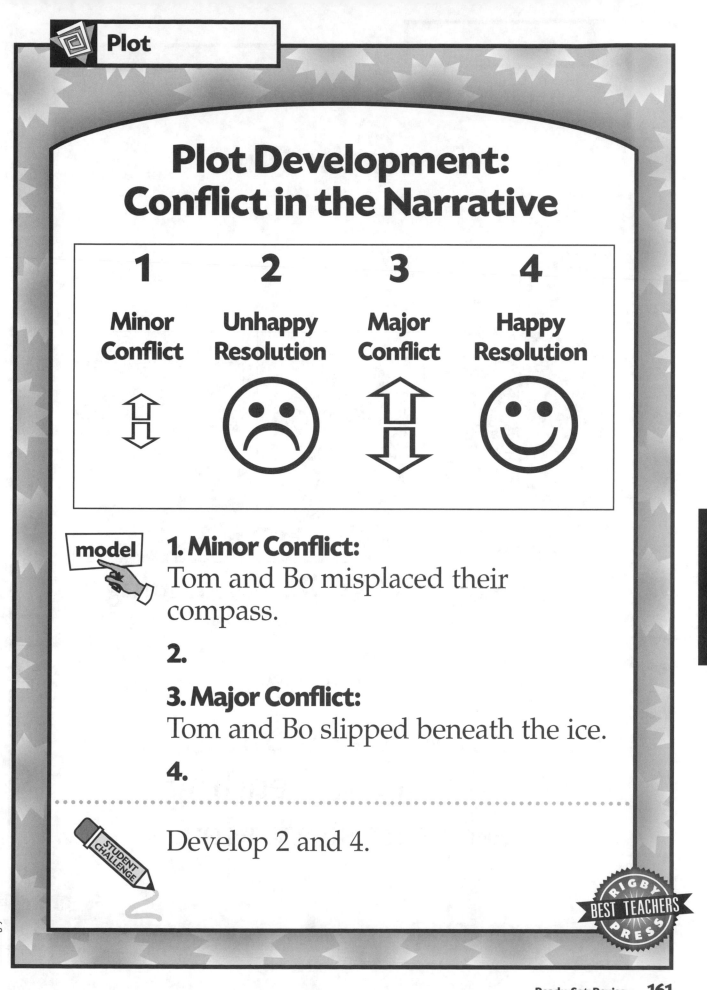

1. Minor Conflict:
Tom and Bo misplaced their compass.

2.

3. Major Conflict:
Tom and Bo slipped beneath the ice.

4.

Develop 2 and 4.

Draw the Plot

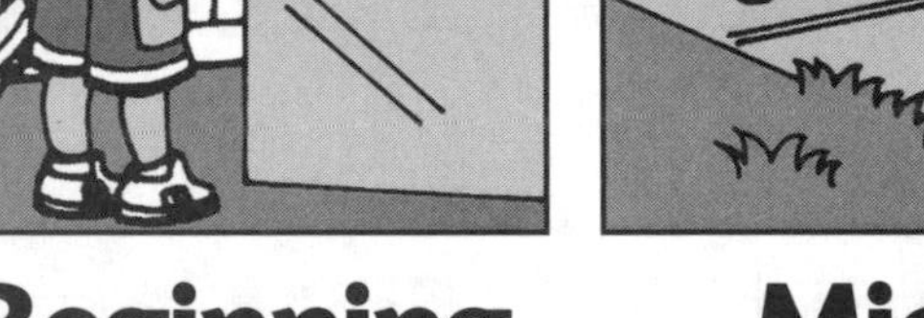

Beginning **Middle** **Ending**

Draw a beginning, middle, and ending for your story idea.

Connect the Events

- Charlie's bike needs a new tire.
- Aunt Meg is painting her house.
- Justin has just returned from summer camp.

When Justin returned from summer camp, he found things just as he had left them. Aunt Meg was outside painting the house and Charlie's bike still was in need of a new tire.

Write a scene that connects three seemingly unrelated events.

Plot

Teaching Points

Elaboration

Supporting with Examples

Opinion:
If you want to be a good athlete, drink milk.

Persuasive Reason:
Milk is a major source of calcium, which is needed for strong bones.

Supporting Example:
Patrick Ewing drinks a glass of milk every day.

Opinion:
People should not litter.

Write a persuasive reason and a supporting example for this opinion.

Show vs. Tell

He ate dinner.

Gary devoured the mashed potatoes covered with golden streams of melted butter.

He sat in the chair.

Elaboration

Interesting!

The door was stuck.

Mary Ann twisted the doorknob and shoved with all her might, but the door would not budge.

The cookie tasted good.

No Explanation Needed

Scott is bored.

His eyes are half closed.

He repeatedly glances at the clock.

He drums the tabletop with his hands.

Use physical clues to show how a character feels.

Daniel is ashamed.

Character Development

Maggie sat on the hard lump in the middle of the back seat. The sunlight streamed in harshly from the left window.

Maggie sat on the hard lump in the middle of the back seat, pressed tightly between Sarah and Jackie. The sunlight streamed in harshly from the left window, even though she couldn't see out of it. "Sisters, who needs them?" thought Maggie.

Steven sat quietly on the boat waiting for his turn to ski.

The Conflict: Situation Needs Improvement

The classroom desks are in disrepair.

I can't think about multiplying percents when my desk wobbles every time I move. Mrs. Johansen doesn't even seem to notice that the broken leg on my chair makes a tap, tap, tap sound when I try to erase a mistake.

The classroom is overcrowded.

The Conflict: Person in Trouble

Bryan did not pass the math test.

Rather than study fractions, Bryan stayed up all night helping his mother unpack the last of the moving cartons.

Molly is afraid of the water.

Sensory Details

smell
texture
taste
sound
sight

Feeling the warmth of the campfire, Becca inhaled the crisp night air and relaxed under a canopy of golden autumn leaves.

Write a sensory experience sentence.

Sensory Details: Smell

Mom hugged me.

Gathered in Mom's loving arms, I was also embraced by the smell of her favorite perfume.

The air smells different just before a storm.

Sensory Details: Taste

The cake was sweet.

Custard cream spilled out from the spongy sweetness of the cake, and the crumb topping dissolved into a sugary decadence.

Write a sentence focusing on taste about one of the following:

- **cotton candy**
- **ketchup on fries**
- **steak from the grill**
- **other favorite food**

Sensory Details: Touch

The bed was cold.

My toes stood at attention as I slid them beneath the stiff cold sheets.

Write a sentence focusing on touch about one of the following:

- **new denim jeans**
- **a kitten**
- **sunburned skin**

Sensory Details: Sight

The forest is beautiful.

Golden shafts of light poured down through the dew-laden green leaves, reaching the droplets of mist on the earthen floor.

Write a sentence focusing on sight about one of the following:

- **the desk**
- **your shoe**
- **the window**
- **a dog**

Sensory Details: Sound

The birds chirped.

Birds, trilling sweetly, filled the morning sky with the silken flutter of wings.

Write a sentence focusing on sound about one of the following:

- **bees**
- **the library**
- **a volcano erupting**

Memory Details

I remember standing on tiptoe peeking through the railing of the crib, wondering how such an earsplitting noise could come from that tiny mouth.

Describe a childhood memory.

Reflection Creates Personal Tone

I... wish
hope
dream
wonder
if only...

I wonder if he knew how frightened I was as I stood inside the airlock, imagining the fate awaiting me.

Create personal tone by reflecting on a possibility.

Elaboration by Example

A fond memory is sitting in Grandma's kitchen smelling the wafting Thanksgiving feast, while my aunts chatted and laughed about things I did not yet understand.

Elaborate on a funny memory using an example.

Elaboration by Comparison

Fond memories warm you like a cup of cocoa sipped in front of the fire.

Elaborate on a funny memory using comparison.

Elaboration by Function

Fond memories give us strength and joy throughout our lives.

Elaborate on a funny memory using function.

Supporting with Comparison

- State comparison between item A and item B
- Develop
  item A looks, acts, does
  item B looks, acts, does
- Conclusion

Hurricanes and tornadoes both are destructive tempests. Hurricanes are larger and last longer; however, tornadoes can be more devastating since they often occur without much warning. The awesome power of these storms causes tremendous damage each year.

Compare two sports.

Support with Definition

Enunciation, the act of speaking clearly and effectively, is fundamental to public speaking. A speaker who slurs his words or mumbles will quickly lose his audience.

A nutritious lunch makes you feel good.

Elaboration

Support with Facts and Statistics

A lot of students failed the math test.

Ten of the twenty students in the class failed the math test.

Most students bring their lunch to school.

Support with Quotations

This year's sixth grade class has outstanding musical ability. Mrs. Jones, our music teacher, observed, "This is the most talented group in the school."

Use a quotation to support a statement about a friend's soccer ability.

Support with Anecdote

Mrs. Main is a generous teacher.

When Susan forgot her lunch, Mrs. Main shared her own lunch. She told Susan it was no trouble at all.

Heather is an unfriendly student.

Persuasive Writing: Loaded Words

Blinky Burgers give you the energy to live a fuller life.

or

Tinsel Toothpaste whitens your teeth to give you a dazzling smile.

Write a persuasive sentence using loaded words.

Persuasive Writing: Ordinary Folks

As a person who loves to read, I can assure you *Charlotte's Web* is a wonderful novel. The characters are unforgettable, and the story is touching and funny.

Elaborate as an ordinary person persuading others to try out for the track team.

Persuasive Writing: Comparison

Charlotte's Web is written with more delightful detail than the book *The Spider Sat*.

Elaborate with comparison to persuade others to root for one team over another.

Persuasive Writing: Endorsement

Charlotte's Web is an award-winning book recommended by the American Library Association.

Use an endorsement from a respected organization or well-known person to sell energy bars.

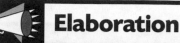

Persuasive Writing: Bandwagon

All students at Southside School have read *Charlotte's Web*.

Use the bandwagon approach to convince others to recycle.

Persuasive Writing: Fact

Why should you eat properly and exercise?

People who eat healthy and exercise have fewer medical problems.

Why should you save money for the future?

Persuasive Writing: Example

Why should you eat properly and exercise?

Hannah reduced her blood pressure by doing aerobic exercise three times a week and cutting out fatty foods.

Why should you save money for the future?

Persuasive Writing: Expert Opinion

Why should you eat properly and exercise?

The Tri-County Doctors Association states that eating healthy and exercising can increase life expectancy.

Why should you save money for the future?

Persuasive Writing: Emotional Plea

Why should you eat properly and exercise?

I don't want you to get sick.

Why should you save money for the future?

Persuasive Writing: Logic

Why should you eat properly and exercise?

Since healthy diet and fitness activities help increase life expectancy and quality of life, why wouldn't you eat healthy and exercise?

Why should you save money for the future?

RIGBY
BEST TEACHERS
PRESS

model

STUDENT CHALLENGE